Gearhead Garage

CHOPPERS

PETER BODENSTEINER

BLACK
RABBIT
BOOKS

Bolt is published by Black Rabbit Books
P.O. Box 3263, Mankato, Minnesota, 56002.
www.blackrabbitbooks.com
Copyright © 2017 Black Rabbit Books

Design and Production by Michael Sellner
Photo Research by Rhonda Milbrett

Library of Congress Control Number: 2015954670

HC ISBN: 978-1-68072-028-0   PB ISBN: 978-1-68072-258-1

Printed in the United States at CG Book Printers,
North Mankato, Minnesota, 56003. PO #1790 4/16

Web addresses included in this book were working and appropriate
at the time of publication. The publisher is not responsible for broken
or changed links.

BOLT

CONTENTS

CHAPTER 1

Fast and Loud

The rider throws his leg over the chopper. He kicks it to a start. The motorcycle rumbles to life. He twists the handlebar grip. The motorcycle roars and pops.

Everyone nearby turns to watch. The rider steers his bike toward the road. He **revs** the engine again and speeds off.

Known for Being Different

The roar of a chopper motorcycle is a powerful sound. It's one thing choppers are known for. They are also known for being fast. But every chopper looks different. And that's what makes them cool. People take **stock** motorcycles and change them. They make them look however they want.

Choppers have long or short handlebars. They can have fat or skinny tires.

Safety Helmet Laws in North America

Bikers over age 21 are required to wear helmets in these areas.

Canada

Washington

Vermont

Massachusetts

New Jersey

Maryland

New York

Virginia

North Carolina

West Virginia

Georgia

Tennessee

Alabama

Mississippi

Louisiana

Missouri

Nebraska

United States

Mexico

Nevada

Oregon

California

CHAPTER 2

The  of Choppers

Motorcycles were invented in the 1800s. They became popular quickly. Soldiers even used them during war.

During World War II, U.S. soldiers rode fast motorcycles in **Europe**. After the war, they wanted to make their bikes at home faster. They removed parts from stock bikes. Taking off parts made the bikes lighter. These bikes were called bobbers. Bobbers had a simple, clean look.

70%

Chopping Them Up

In the 1960s, people started really changing motorcycles. They started cutting the **frames**. Then they would **weld** them back together in new ways.

With these frames, builders made lower and longer bikes. These builders were "chopping up" bikes to make new ones. And that's where the name "chopper" came from.

More than half of U.S. states require motorcycle drivers to wear eye protection.

Choppers Today

Today, choppers are more popular than ever. Companies sell parts just for building choppers. These parts let more people build **unique** bikes. They also make building custom bikes easier.

Movies and TV have helped make choppers popular. TV programs show viewers how choppers are built.

Building Custom Bikes

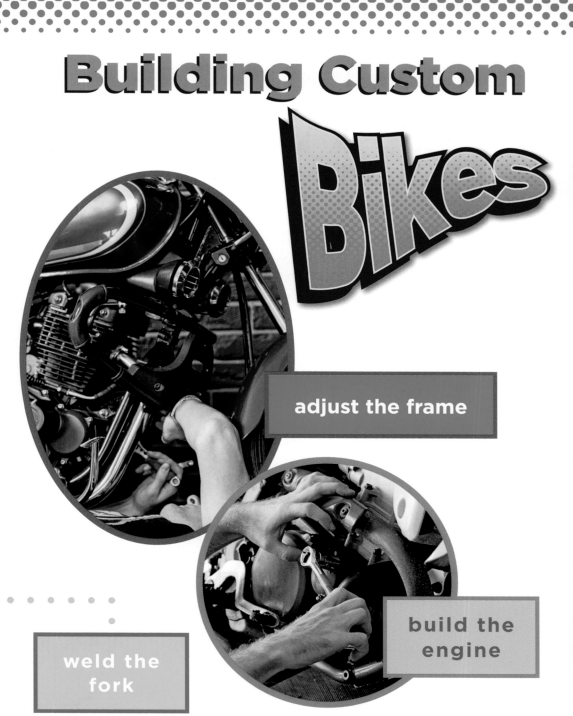

adjust the frame

build the engine

weld the fork

CHAPTER 3

Building a Chopper

Chopper builders can create whatever a customer wants. Many people want handlebars that look cool. Tall handlebars that go above a rider's shoulders are called ape hangers. These handlebars make steering hard. But they give the bike a unique look.

Tires and Forks

Tires and forks make choppers different too. Some choppers have fat rear tires and skinny front tires. But riders can choose whatever tires they like best.

Forks connect tires to the handlebars. Many choppers have very long forks. Forks are often the most expensive parts of choppers.

One of the most famous choppers is the "Captain America." It was used in the movie *Easy Rider*. Many people copied that chopper's design.

CHOPPER PARTS

SKINNY FRONT TIRE

FORKS

APE HANGER
HANDLEBARS

FAT
REAR TIRE

GAS TANK

FRAME

Chopper Art

Building choppers is now an art form. Bikes often have fancy paint jobs. Riders want shiny **chrome** parts. They also want loud **exhaust** pipes.

Custom parts are expensive. Choppers can cost $50,000 or more to build.

CHAPTER 4

The Future of Choppers

Choppers are very popular now. Some people feel they are too common. Some have returned to simple styles from the past. Many people are building bobbers again. Others are building choppers that look like 1960s café racers.

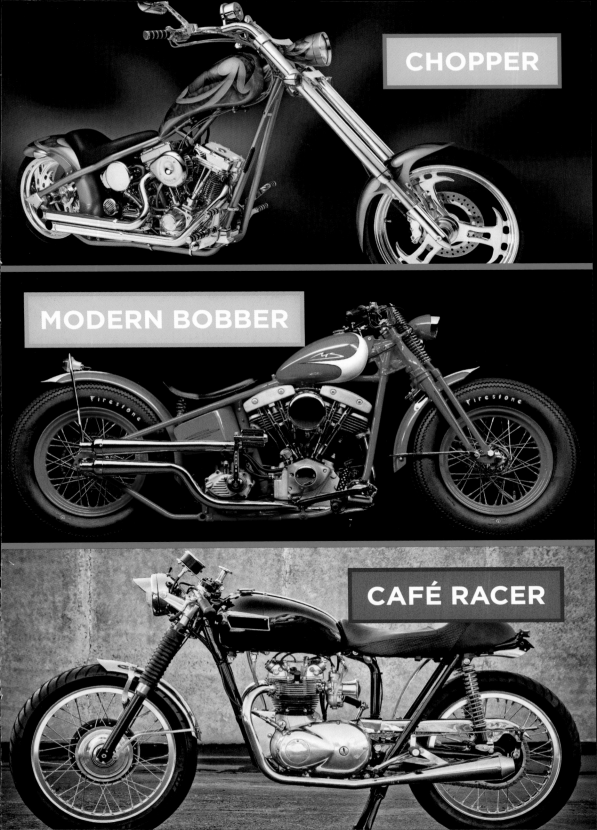

CHOPPER

MODERN BOBBER

CAFÉ RACER

One-of-a-Kind Bikes

Some people won't settle for stock motorcycles. They want something louder or faster. New technology, such as 3D printing, will help builders make more unique parts.

No one knows what the future of choppers will be. But they'll always be one-of-a-kind bikes.

1903

Harley-Davidson Motor Company is founded.

1940s

Bikers start making bobbers.

1969

Easy Rider sparks interest in choppers.

1900

World War II ends.

1945

The first people walk on the moon.

1969

1990s

Drivers begin to focus on custom paint jobs.

2003

American Chopper TV show begins.

2005

The Mount St. Helens volcano erupts.

1980

Terrorists attack the World Trade Center and Pentagon.

2001

chrome (KROM)—a metal used to cover other metals in order to make them shiny

Europe (YUR-up)—the sixth largest continent

exhaust (ig-ZOST)—the mixture of gases produced by an engine

frame (FRAYM)—the structure that supports the body of a motorcycle or automobile

rev (REV)—to cause an engine to run more quickly

stock (STAHK)—usually available for sale in a store

unique (yoo-NEEK)—very special or unusual

weld (WELD)—to join pieces of metal together by heating the edges until they melt and then pressing them together

BOOKS

David, Jack. *Choppers.* Motorcycles. Minneapolis: Bellwether Media, 2008.

Ingram, Kevin. *Motorcycles.* Wonderwise: Mankato, MN: Smart Apple Media, 2016.

Riggs, Kate. *Motorcycles.* Seedlings. Mankato, MN: Creative Education, 2015.

WEBSITES

12 Motorcycles That Trace the Evolution of the All-American Chopper
www.wired.com/2015/02/12-motorcycles-trace-evolution-american-chopper/

A Brief History of Motorcycling
www.nhtsa.gov/people/injury/pedbimot/motorcycle/00-NHT-212-motorcycle/history5-6.html

Building a Chopper Chassis
www.youtube.com/watch?v=aSAwKLiBLMU

INDEX